John Wooden: The Inspiring Life and Leadership Lessons of One of Basketball's Greatest Coaches

An Unauthorized Biography & Leadership Case Study

By: Clayton Geoffreys

Table of Contents

Foreword

Once every generation, there is a coach who transcends everyone else. For much of the 20th century, that basketball coach was John Wooden. In his career, Wooden led the UCLA team to ten national championships, including one run that ran for seven consecutive years. More importantly though, Wooden was known for more than just being a basketball coach, but also building up his players to live meaningful and fulfilling lives beyond the game of basketball. He was in many ways more than a coach, but also a friend, mentor, and leader. Thank you for purchasing *John Wooden: The Inspiring Life and Leadership Lessons of One of Basketball's Greatest Coaches*. In this unauthorized biography and leadership case study, we will learn some of the background behind John Wooden's incredible life story, and more importantly his impact on the game of basketball. In the last section of the book, we'll learn what makes John Wooden such an effective leader and coach, including a review of key takeaways that you can remember when looking to apply lessons from John Wooden to your own life. Hope you enjoy and if you do, please do not forget to leave a review!

Also, check out my website at claytongeoffreys.com to join my exclusive list where I let you know about my latest books. To thank you for your purchase, you can go to my site to download a free copy of *33 Life Lessons: Success Principles, Career Advice & Habits of Successful People*. In the book, you'll learn from some of the greatest thought leaders of different industries on what it takes to become successful and how to live a great life.

Cheers,

Clayton Geoffreys

Visit me at www.claytongeoffreys.com

Introduction

It is often said that we walk in the footsteps of our forebears. The world is built by men and women that have been inspired by people that came before them. We develop on what others before us have started, and we work on it to make it better or pave the way for other generations to start on where we left off. That is the endless cycle of how society and any discipline progresses.

The same is true in the world of basketball. The players of today were shaped by the eras of yesterday. Today's players work on the skills that past legends honed and used as their trademark moves to make them unique or to perfect them in ways that yesterday's stars were not able to do. That is how the game of basketball evolves. Skills, knowledge, and nutrition improve as players today study what has happened to the basketball stars that have played in the years or decades before them.

In the lore of basketball knowledge and strategy, the legendary coaches that have become household names these past two decades worked similarly on what their forebears started long before they even knew the X's and O's of the sport. Luke Walton learned from Steve Kerr. Steve Kerr had the pleasure of playing under two legends in the likes of Phil Jackson and Gregg Popovich. And when you trace it all the way back, perhaps all the coaches that have been avid students of the game can trace their roots down to the legendary John Wooden's teachings.

John Wooden's name is usually synonymous with the UCLA basketball dynasty during the 60's and 70's. He was the man responsible for bringing home the NCAA championship to Westwood ten times in only 12 years, thus earning him the nickname "The Wizard of Westwood." And during those 12 years, he won the title for the UCLA Bruins a record seven times while other coaches could not even win three national titles in a row in Division I basketball. When it came down to winning during that era of college basketball, nobody did it better than Wooden.

With the way Wooden led the Bruins in that 12-year dominance in college basketball, many have come to admire and follow the path that the legendary coach has paved. No real student of basketball has never read about John Wooden and his philosophies and teachings that have been passed down from generation to generation. UCLA players that have played under him, such as Kareem Abdul-Jabbar and Bill Walton, have all made it a point to pass on what they have learned from Wooden. Most notably, Bill Walton is one of the most beloved followers of the coach and even passed on the same philosophies to his son Luke, who was an assistant coach for the Golden State Warriors and is now the head coach of the Los Angeles Lakers.

But Wooden's influence was not limited to what his former players passed down. In his book entitled "Pyramid of Success," John Wooden has earned millions of followers all over the world for the teachings he has imparted with the words he wrote. Athletes who have never met him or played under him suddenly became avid believers and followers. Both Kobe Bryant and LeBron James grew up reading about Wooden's work. Stephen Curry of the Golden State Warriors was influenced by how his head coach Steve Kerr and his general manager Bob Myers built their championship teams based on Wooden's Pyramid of Success. And when it came to successful coaches, Mike Krzyzewski built his success at Duke University and as the head coach of USA Basketball based on what he learned from Wooden.

As good of a basketball coach and inspirational figure of success as Wooden has become, his influence was never limited to the sport he excelled in. In the world of entertainment, actors such as Tom Hanks and Matthew McConaughey were avid fans of John Wooden. Even athletes of other sports have come to identify their success with the teachings of Wooden.

These athletes include Drew Brees of the New Orleans Saints and Derek Jeter of the New York Yankees. Even notable names in the world of leadership and business such as Barack Obama, Bill Gates, George W. Bush, and John Maxwell have learned a thing or two from how John Wooden built a world of success on basketball.

Though John Wooden's philosophies of success may have transcended the world of basketball and penetrated the realms of other sports and businesses as well, he is still most beloved and revered for what he contributed to the sport he helped make as popular as it is today. He was one of the first great guards in the history of the sport and was a great mind as a head coach to become the first person in history to be enshrined in the Basketball Hall of Fame both as a player and coach. And because of how he became arguably the most successful player and coach in college basketball, an award was named in his honor.

The John R. Wooden Award is an annual awards program that honors the most outstanding players and coaches of men's and women's college basketball. Through the John R. Wooden Award, the All-American Teams are selected. And from those teams, the Players of the Year for both men and women's college basketball are determined. Meanwhile, the Legends of Coaching Award is an annual honor given to coaches that have shown the same kind of success and dedication to the game of basketball as John Wooden did.

Because of his influence as a basketball mentor and coach and as a transcendent figure when it comes to success, John Wooden has become one of the pioneers that have paved the way for the success of today's coaches, players, and leaders. He has become so revered and important to the world of basketball that his name has become almost as legendary as James Naismith, the man who invented the sport. And when you factor in how he influenced the world outside of basketball, he may even be considered a more important figure.

Chapter 1: Background

It was no surprise that basketball would become John Wooden's passion and ticket to success. He was born in Hall, Indiana back on October 14, 1910. While Indiana would soon be known as a basketball state because of how its citizens are crazy about the sport, basketball was not yet as big there as it is today. Back in 1910, basketball was still in its early stages.

John Wooden's parents, Joshua Hugh and Roxie Anne, raised the future basketball legend during difficult times. While living on a farm, John grew up without any electricity or even running water. And more often than not, Joshua and Roxie struggled to keep food on the table because of how scarce their money supply was back then.[i] The young John Wooden would make life easier for his family by helping out with the chores. He would wake up early in the morning to help milk the cows and do whatever farm chores he was asked to do.[ii]

Because Indiana was one of the first states that embraced the sport of basketball at its early stages, John Wooden played a lot of it back when he was still a child in a limited form. He and his brothers, Maurice, Daniel, and William, would make a homemade version of a ball and would shoot it through one of the baskets that they used on their farm.[ii] This was one of the many ways that John Wooden passed his time as a young boy after doing his farm chores and schoolwork.

However, more difficulties struck the Wooden family in the 1920's. Rural communities and towns in America were hard-pressed to keep up with the economic instabilities of that era. Thus, John Wooden's family lost their farm to bankruptcy and were forced to move out of Hall to Martinsville, Indiana. While it was a stroke of bad luck that had his family moved away from his childhood home, living in Martinsville helped John in eventually forging his legendary status in basketball.

As basketball was evolving and becoming more popular, the Indiana began to embrace the sport more than any other state in America back in the 1920's. Basketball had one of its best moments in history when Reverend Nicholas McKay brought the sport to Indiana in the early period of the century. It became so popular that the state began a high school tournament in 1911. By the 1920's, the tournaments were already so popular that thousands of fans would watch the games to cheer rabidly for their teams. And when James Naismith, the inventor of basketball, went to one of the high school tournaments, he said that it had its origin in Indiana though it was invented in Springfield, Massachusetts. Naismith even said that Indiana remained the center of basketball.[iii]

Indiana, a basketball-crazy state, was the right place for Wooden to grow up. The then-14-year-old John Wooden's popularity as a young high school guard skyrocketed when the family moved to Martinsville, where he had more opportunity to shine. Wooden began to make a name for himself as an equally skilled guard for Martinsville High School while idolizing an Indiana high school basketball legend, Robert "Fuzzy" Vandivier of Franklin High School. For three straight years, he led Martinsville to consecutive appearances in the state championship tournament. He won the title twice during that period. And during those three years, Wooden was an All-State selection.[iv]

In 1928, John Wooden would attend Purdue University in West Lafayette, Indiana. He would major in civil engineering at first but decided to study English later while playing stellar basketball for the university. Standing 5'10", Wooden was a star guard for Purdue and earned his popularity because of how quick he played in that era. And because John Wooden was never afraid of contact and would easily get up after a rough dive for the ball, he was given his first nickname, the "Indiana Rubber Man."[v]

Wooden would earn three consecutive All-American selections from 1929 to 1932 as a Purdue Boilermaker. At one point, he was named college player of the year decades before that award was named after him. And in 1932, the Boilermakers would win the national title before the first NCAA champions were crowned in 1939. Several decades later, the 1932 Purdue Boilermakers led by John Wooden would retroactively be declared the NCAA champions of that year.[ii]

Chapter 2: Coaching Career

Early Coaching Jobs

After leaving Purdue University with a degree in English and as one of its most distinguished basketball stars, John Wooden would live a life as a teacher in Kentucky at Dayton High School. Two years later, he would return to Indiana in South Bend to continue his career as a teacher while coaching high school sports and playing professional basketball.

While teaching and coaching, John Wooden played professionally for the Indiana Kautskys (later known as the Indianapolis Jets) of the Basketball Association of America. Wooden spurned several lucrative offers from other teams because he wanted to play for Indiana. However, at that time, basketball was not the most popular sport. It was risky because America was still recovering from the Great Depression while relations with other countries were also seeing low points. Because of this, Wooden was only earning

$2,000 on an annual basis as a professional player. He was paid $50 for every game he played.

It was a different landscape back then. Today and over the last five decades, a player had to pour all of their time and effort to their professional team. Playing professionally is a basketball player's primary source of income. However, during Wooden's time, basketball was merely a secondary means of income for him and his family. His primary jobs were teaching and coaching.

As a teacher and coach first and a player second, John Wooden inspired his students and players to believe that academics and sports were more than just the sum of what their grades and the scoreboard said. He taught that learning and development was the better product of academics and sports, and it was only through working hard that a person could achieve success. It was then and there during his stay in South Bend when John Wooden developed his Pyramid of Success.[ii]

John Wooden would take a break from his teaching and coaching career when World War II struck. In 1942, he would serve the United States as a Navy lieutenant. He would serve the Navy for two years before returning to the world of basketball. He could not extend his service because of appendicitis. While an inflamed appendix is never a good thing, Wooden was lucky that it prevented him from getting shipped to the South Pacific because the officer that replaced his post was killed during the attack on Pearl Harbor.[i] The world would have been robbed of what would eventually be one of the most prominent figures in basketball and success.

Coaching at Indiana State University

John Wooden would return from military service but was not re-hired by South Bend High School. However, he quickly found employment as the basketball coach at Indiana State Teachers College (now known as Indiana State University) in Terre Haute, Indiana.

Wooden would continue teaching while part-timing as a coach for the baseball team during his stay at Indiana State.

Indiana State became a successful program under John Wooden. In only his first season with the team, ISU went 18-8. They would go on to win the Indiana Collegiate Conference Title that season and the team was invited to participate in the National Association of Intercollegiate Basketball Tournament held in Kansas City. However, Wooden declined the invitation.

The NAIB prohibited black players from participating in their tournament. Being a man that loved his team and players more than anything, Wooden refused to accept the invitation because they could not bring one of their players, a young man named Clarence Walker. For John Wooden, it never mattered what the color of your skin was. What mattered most was that the player worked hard for success. Saying that Walker was not one of the guys that got to play a lot of minutes,

Wooden still regarded him as a part of the team nonetheless, and ISU would not be complete without him.[vi]

The following season, ISU would again win the conference title after posting a 27-7 record and would be invited to the NAIB Tournament for the second year in a row. This time, the NAIB relaxed the rules and allowed Walker to play in the tournament. However, he was not initially allowed to stay with the team in the same hotel. That did not sit well with Wooden.

After a little persuasion, they would later allow Clarence Walker to play and stay with the team throughout the tournament. In a show of solidarity, the team would not go anywhere that did not permit African-Americans. Clarence Walker, who would work as a school guidance counselor, would make history by being the first African-American player to play in a national collegiate tournament. It was all thanks to John Wooden's stance on the matter.[vi]

The Purdue University product would lead the team to a 44-15 record in the two seasons he spent with them. And in those two years, they won the Indiana Collegiate Conference Title back-to-back and were invited to the NAIB Tournament twice. They would make it all the way to the finals in the 1948 tournament but would end up losing to Louisville. The defeat marked the only time in his life that John Wooden lost a championship game. It also turned out that Wooden would no longer be coaching ISU after that.

The Move to Westwood

In 1948, John Wooden would receive two new coaching offers. The first one was from the University of Minnesota. The second proposal was from the University of California, Los Angeles. As enticing as the UCLA offer was, Wooden was leaning towards accepting the Minnesota offer because he liked the idea of staying in the Midwest instead of going all the way to Southern California.

When the deadline to make his decision came, John Wooden did not get a call from the University of Minnesota. He initially thought that they had lost interest in him, but it would turn out that they could not reach him due to inclement weather. Thinking that he had no offers left, Wooden would give his word to UCLA to become their new head coach. Minnesota tried to convince him otherwise, but Wooden told them that he could no longer change his mind after giving UCLA his word.[vii]

John Wooden would find that coaching the UCLA Bruins was a tough challenge early on. The Bruins were considered the worst team in the Pacific conference. What was worse was that the Westwood-based University lacked the proper facilities to make the team competitive. They had to share practice facilities with the school's other teams. What was worse was that they did not have an on-campus arena. At one point, their home games had to be played at neighboring schools.

But John Wooden never gave up amidst the early challenges he faced. Preaching discipline and hard work, he would coach the Bruins to surprise everyone in the region. UCLA went 22-7 in Wooden's first season as the head coach to silence skeptics and critics that said that the Bruins were the worst team in the Pacific. They would even go on to win the Pacific Conference title in John Wooden's first season as the head coach.

The next season, John Wooden would prove that his UCLA Bruins were not one-hit wonders. He would surpass the 22-win season he had a year before by going for 24 wins during the 1949-50 season. Wooden would secure another division title for the school. They would win the overall conference title for the second year in a row. Before his arrival, UCLA had only won two conference titles. But in only two years, Wooden had already tied that mark.

John Wooden and the UCLA Bruins would continue to dominate the Pacific Conference during the 50's. They would win the conference titles again in 1952 and 1956. It was during the 1956 season when the Bruins won 17 straight games and went undefeated to win the conference title. But in the NCAA Tournament, they would see their winning streak end at the hands of the University of San Francisco, which had the legendary Bill Russell.

But no matter how good Wooden's Bruins were, they had little to no success in the NCAA Tournament. The Bruins would only make the tournament three times from 1948 to 1960. And in those three appearances, UCLA and John Wooden would get eliminated in only the first round of the NCAA Tournament. UCLA's fate did not get any better when the school was placed on probation after a recruitment scandal. And during that time, the University of California, Berkeley took control of the Pacific Conference after the UCLA Bruins had dominated it for much of the 50's.

Making the Final Four, the Beginning of the Dominant Run

After the 1960 season ended, the UCLA Bruins finished the season with a 14-12 record. That was John Wooden's worst record as the head coach of the Bruins. The soon-to-be legendary coach would get back to the drawing board to contemplate what went wrong that season. He would conclude that the Bruins tended to lose their punch and energy in the latter parts of the season.

John Wooden thought that the reason why his teams would usually start losing late in the season was that he had been pushing them hard and that the bench did not mesh well with the starters. This prompted him to tweak his practices a little bit by rotating bench players with the starters during scrimmages. This led to an improvement in how players handled fatigue and how the bench players played together with the starters.[viii]

During the 1961-62 season, John Wooden got the UCLA Bruins back to the top of the conference after the probation had been lifted. The reassurance that John Wooden gave the program back in 1960 all came to fruition. That little tweak he made turned the Bruins into a powerhouse squad that might have been the best the school had seen up to that point in time. For the first time in Wooden's stint as the Bruins' head coach, UCLA got out of the first round of the NCAA Tournament and made it all the way to the Final Four.

That dominant run in the NCAA Tournament would secure UCLA a battle against Cincinnati in the semi-finals. The Bruins might have made it all the way to the NCAA finals if it were not for a controversial foul call that gave Cincinnati the win and the championship berth that year. Cincinnati would eventually win the national championships that season after that close win against the UCLA Bruins in the semi-finals.

After that game against Cincinnati, John Wooden told his players the best thing they could hear from a head coach. He never told them the errors they committed or even the setbacks that led them to that loss. He hardly even talked about winning as the measuring tape of success for the Bruins. Instead, John Wooden told the team that they had already proved that they could play with the best of the best that the country had to offer.[viii]

The UCLA Bruins would not have the best season the following year, but it did not stop John Wooden from believing that the best was yet to come. He would foretell the coming of the 1964 championship, especially considering that his starters were Walt Hazzard, Fred Slaughter, Keith Erickson, Jack Hirsch, and the legendary Gail Goodrich, who would later forge a Hall of Fame career in the NBA.

With challenges that included playing outside of the campus because of the school's lack of facilities, the UCLA Bruins were never considered a favorite. What was worse than their lack of facilities was that the Bruins were an undersized team. At that time, the center position was the difference-maker. Bill Russell led San Francisco to a national title on the strength of his size advantage and defensive prowess. But the 1963-64 Bruins did not have anybody of that size. Their tallest player was the 6'7" backup center, Doug McIntosh. Their starting center, Fred Slaughter, was only 6'5". But John Wooden never allowed the externalities affect their play.

Jerry Norman, one of Wooden's players in two of his teams at UCLA, was working as an assistant for UCLA. While Norman may be loyal to the Bruins, he was a big fan of Pete Newell, who coached Cal against UCLA in many battles and is one of only a few coaches in basketball history to have a winning record against John Wooden. Norman liked the idea of how

Newell believed that controlling the pace of the game meant controlling the game itself.

One of the many influences that Jerry Norman had on John Wooden was that he convinced the UCLA legend to control the tempo of the game and force turnovers for a fast-paced scoring style by using a zone press. Despite UCLA's lack of size in the middle, they had a lot of sprinters and quick perimeter players with long arms that could force turnovers and finish the break in a hurry.[viii]

With UCLA playing a fast-paced game that loved to force turnovers, the Bruins looked unstoppable during the 1963-64 season under John Wooden. The entire team played an inspired style of basketball that looked disarranged because of the pressing defense but was still in harmony. Their defensive style forced blitzes and runs that would soon earn the name "Bruin Blitz."

The UCLA Bruins would blitz all the way to an undefeated path towards the NCAA Tournament. And even the best programs all over the country were no match for John Wooden's Bruins. Most notably, it was a second-half blitz against San Francisco that brought them to the NCAA Final Four, the farthest they had reached at that point under John Wooden.

In the Final Four, they would manage to fight a tight game against Kansas, a school that seemed like a home team throughout the entire tournament. But after seeing themselves down by five points in the final five minutes of the game, UCLA had one of its blitzes and scored 11 points in only three minutes. With that run, Coach John Wooden had beaten Kansas State and was on his way to the national championship game for the first time in his career.

An inspired UCLA team never slowed down against Duke University in the national championship game. After seeing themselves down by a few points in the first half, the Bruins would go on a run that made it seem like UCLA was destined to win the title that year.

They were much smaller compared to the 6'10" towers that Duke had in the paint. But the Bruins used their speed and discipline to play the style that brought them to the dance. After a total of 29 forced turnovers, the UCLA Bruins were crowned the new NCAA champions of that season. All that John Wooden could tell his players was that they must act like champions.

In 1965, John Wooden retained the majority of what made the UCLA Bruins champions. They still had Gail Goodrich, Kenny Washington, and Doug McIntosh. Though they did not finish the season undefeated, they were still the title favorites heading into the championship game against Michigan. They would repeat as national champions while Gail Goodrich was named College Player of the Year of that season.

The following year, John Wooden would lose the core of his back-to-back championship teams. However, UCLA still kept the same discipline and system that helped them dominate the college ranks the last two years. They would finish the season 18-8 but would not qualify for the NCAA Tournament because they failed to win the conference title to Oregon State.

After a one-year break from the championship picture, John Wooden would coach UCLA all the way back to dominance when Lew Alcindor (now known as Kareem Abdul-Jabbar) would get elevated to varsity after looking like a man among boys on the freshman team. The 7'2" future NBA all-time great was so dominant in the middle of the paint that the UCLA Bruins looked a lot different from the guard-oriented and fast-paced team that dominated the country three years ago.

With John Wooden at the helm coaching a UCLA team that had Lew Alcindor dominating the middle to the point that the NCAA banned the dunk, the Bruins would go for another undefeated season on their way to their return to the national championship game against Dayton. After only a season of ceding the NCAA title to another team, UCLA would regain their place at the top of the collegiate mountain by defeating Dayton.

As the future Abdul-Jabbar was entering his junior year in college, UCLA were still favorites to win the national title, especially with how incredibly dominant the 7'2" center was under John Wooden's tutelage. But Big Lew was not a mere one-man wrecking crew. Wooden's successful teams always banked on their all-around effort. And because of that, the 1967-68 UCLA Bruins won 17 straight games before entering one of the most high profile matchups in college basketball history.

John Wooden coached the Bruins to 47 straight wins spanning from the last season on their way to what was dubbed as the "Game of the Century." As basketball was getting more and more popular, the college game had also seen an increase in followers. In the first nationally televised college basketball game, UCLA would face off against the University of Houston.

Wooden's UCLA Bruins were led by big Lew Alcindor in the middle. However, Houston had their own dominant big man. While Elvin Hayes was merely 6'9" compared to Abdul-Jabbar at 7'2", he was every bit as dominant and was a candidate for the Player of the Year award, especially with how Houston was just as successful as UCLA throughout the season. In a battle of epic proportions, the smaller Hayes played better than the injured Alcindor as Houston defeated UCLA to end their 47-game winning streak.

After that loss to Houston, John Wooden told the media that UCLA had to start all over again. And true enough, they did. The Bruins would never suffer another defeat after that loss on their way to a rematch with Houston in the Final Four. And with a healthier lineup and revenge on their minds, the Bruins would dominate Houston to avenge their earlier loss. And in the championship game, John Wooden would secure his fourth NCAA title and second back-to-back national title by defeating North Carolina in blowout fashion. That season's UCLA team had dominated the NCAA Tournament so well that four of the All-Tournament team selections were Bruins. It was not a one-man effort on the part of Alcindor since Wooden always preached ball movement and sharing.

During the 1968-69 season, nobody could deny the possibility that UCLA might finish the season as three-peat champions, especially with Lew Alcindor playing in his final year for the Bruins. The Bruins would end the season by winning a title against John Wooden's alma mater, Purdue University, who almost stole him away back in the 50's. Big Lew was named tournament MVP and was leaving UCLA as college basketball's most decorated player of that era. Alcindor, who would later end up as Kareem Abdul-Jabbar and the NBA's all-time leading scorer, would secure John

Wooden his fifth NCAA title and his first three-peat championship.

When Lew Alcindor left UCLA to pursue what would eventually be an all-time great NBA career, the entire nation was relieved, thinking that the collegiate basketball title picture was back to the status quo. However, John Wooden had other things in mind. He would go on to prove that UCLA was more than the sum of its parts and that it was still a powerhouse team despite the loss of their biggest asset.

During the 1969-70 season, the UCLA Bruins banked on holdover veterans such as John Vallely, Curtis Rowe, Henry Bibby, and future NBA All-Star Sidney Wicks. They would rally on the strength of their all-around team play to make it all the way to the NCAA Finals against Jacksonville. Without Lew Alcindor, the UCLA frontline seemed like it would be unable to match up against a gigantic 7'2" Artis Gilmore, who averaged a 20-20 on points and rebounds the entire season. However, the smaller UCLA frontline ganged up on the future NBA All-Star center. With the strength of their defense, the Bruins managed to limit a high-powered Jacksonville offense to win the NCAA title for a fourth straight season. They would finish the season 28-2 to give John Wooden his sixth national title.

John Wooden was able to retain the core players that comprised his championship team for the 1970-71 season. Banking on an even more improved Sidney Wicks and a productive center in Steve Patterson, the Bruins would make it all the way to the NCAA championship game for a fifth straight season. By this time, everybody in the nation already knew that John Wooden had installed a system that lived on despite the graduation of some of his key players. He was an unbeatable head coach that won 29 of UCLA's 30 games that season to win the NCAA title over Villanova.

During the 1971-72 season, John Wooden was excited to field a duo of sophomore players that dominated the freshmen ranks a year before. The biggest name of that pair was a seven-foot center Bill Walton, who excelled in Wooden's system not because of his offense but because of his stellar defensive play and ability to make plays from the post. The other half of that duo was the do-it-all forward Jamaal Wilkes.

On the strength of the Walton-Wilkes tandem, the UCLA Bruins were once again as dominant as they were during Alcindor's time. They were a high-powered offensive team that averaged 95 points a game but only allowed 65 points a night. Because of this, they went on to become undefeated on their way to another NCAA finals berth. Against Florida State in the national championship game, John Wooden had his closest championship game when they defeated their opponents by only five points. And even after winning the title on an undefeated 30-0 season, all that Bill Walton could say was that UCLA did not play well that game. That was how dominant they were and how high they held themselves up under John Wooden's tutelage.

John Wooden's UCLA Bruins never slowed down during the 1972-73 season. They would improve their record win streak to 75 consecutive games after effortlessly going through the competition in the NCAA Tournament. They would beat Memphis State in blowout fashion for their 75th straight win to grab their seventh straight NCAA championship. In that title game, Bill Walton made all but one of the 22 field goals he attempted. He would secure Wooden's eighth NCAA championship.

Both Walton and Wilkes played their final collegiate year during the 1973-74 season. However good the team remained to be, the entire nation stepped up to make the competition a lot tougher. UCLA would nevertheless extend their winning streak to 88 wins. They had never tasted defeat in the Walton era up to that point. However, Notre Dame would play them hard in January of 1974 to end the streak at 88 wins.

Nevertheless, UCLA would reach the NCAA Tournament semis to face North Carolina State. But future NBA star David Thompson's high-powered scoring was too much for the Bruins to handle. When NC State defeated UCLA in the semis, they effectively put an end to the Bruins' reign as the kings of the collegiate ranks. John Wooden's streak as an NCAA championship coach would stop at seven during the Walton-Wilkes duo's senior year. Though Walton and Wilkes would not end their college career in the best circumstances, they would go on to win multiple championships in the NBA as members of some of the great teams during the 80's era.

Come the 1974-75 season, John Wooden's UCLA Bruins were no longer title favorites, especially after they were defeated in the final four the last season. Moreover, he no longer had any star players after

Walton and Wilkes both made their way to the NBA to forge stellar careers as professional basketball players. However, this 1974-75 team was unique because of how Wooden taught them to play a rugged style of defense and an offensive system that was predicated on all-around play.

John Wooden would lead the Bruins to the finals in close fashion when UCLA defeated Louisville in the final four. But after that win, Wooden would announce to the world that he would be coaching his last game in the NCAA finals. He would retire as a coach at age 64. With an inspired group of players wanting to deliver a final title to their head coach, the UCLA Bruins would triumph over the Kentucky Wildcats in the national championship game to make John Wooden the first and only person in the collegiate ranks to win at least ten NCAA championships.

Dave Meyers, the best player on that 1975 championship team, would try his hand at the NBA and would become a part of what was then the biggest trade in history. He was a part of the package that sent former Bruin Kareem Abdul-Jabbar to the Los Angeles Lakers. It was a Bruin for another Bruin since Abdul-Jabbar was now back to the city where he won his first national title. He also found himself closer to where Wooden was.

For Wooden's part, he would finish his 29-year coaching career with a 664-162 record for the UCLA Bruins. He collected a total of ten NCAA championships in only 12 years. And at one point, he won seven straight national titles. No coach has ever won more than three consecutive championships before and after Wooden did it. This only added to John Wooden's reputation as arguably the best coach in college basketball history.

After his coaching career with the UCLA Bruins, John Wooden never coached another basketball game in the collegiate ranks or even the professional realm. He was reported to have been offered a lucrative deal by the Los Angeles Lakers but denied to coach them. However, he would later offer to become an assistant for player development when he was already more than 90 years of age.

It would take another 20 years for UCLA to win another title after John Wooden retired. Several of Wooden's former players and assistants took over the program and posted successful seasons but could not finish the job with a title. They became victims of Wooden's success when UCLA alumni and fans were never satisfied with whatever coach replaced the legendary Wizard of Westwood. And even after that 1995 title, the Bruins would fall into a prolonged drought and would not win another championship since.

Whoever stepped into the head coaching shoes of UCLA would forever live in the shadow of what John Wooden was for the Bruins. This was the reason why no other coach has ever stayed long with the program. Wooden's shoes were always too big for anybody to wear. And for UCLA and the entire collegiate basketball ranks, there has never been a more legendary coach that cast such a large shadow not only over the school but also on the entire basketball world.

John Wooden Award

In 1976, shortly after John Wooden retired, the Wooden award was founded by the John R. Wooden Award Committee to recognize the most outstanding college basketball player every year. There was no better way to give honor to the award than to name it after John Wooden himself, who was college basketball's most celebrated figure and a man that always tried to emphasize that a basketball player should have all the necessary skills of a leader. The first award was given in 1977 to Marques Johnson of UCLA.

Since its inception in 1977, the award has been used to determine the winner every year by a 26-member panel. The top ten out of 20 candidates for the award are selected as members of the All-American Team. And from that team of ten players, only one is distinguished enough to be the recipient of the John Wooden Award. The recipient of the award is considered to be the player that best embodied Wooden's core principles and must be a total package player that has all the necessary skills that Wooden thought to be integral for a successful basketball player.[ix] In 2004, the award was then introduced to the women's division. The first winner was Duke's Alana Beard.

After Marques Johnson was given the inaugural award, several future NBA stars would receive it as well. Larry Bird of Indiana State was the third recipient of the award in 1979. Michael Jordan, who is widely considered to be the greatest of all time, won it in 1984 as a player under Dean Smith's North Carolina Tar

Heels. While playing for the Navy in 1987, David Robinson was another future star that received the award. In 1997, Tim Duncan would win the award for Wake Forest. Kevin Durant, a freshman from Texas, would win it in 2007. And in 2012, Kentucky's Anthony Davis was named the John Wooden Player of the Year.

In 1999, the John Wooden Award Committee would adopt the Legends of Coaching Award, which is a lifetime achievement award given to coaches that embody what John Wooden believed to be the best standards of determining a successful coach. Dean Smith was the inaugural winner of the award in 1999. Other winners include Lute Olson and Mike Krzyzewski.

Death

After living in peace and good health for the majority of his life after retiring from basketball, John Wooden was hospitalized in 2006 and 2007 because of illness in his colon. Despite that, doctors and his daughter still claimed that he was in good physical condition even when he was nearing the age of 100.

On May 26, 2010, John Wooden was sent to the hospital because of dehydration. On June 4 of the same year, he died in the hospital to natural causes. At 99 years old, Wooden would have been a hundred four months later before his death. Several high profile personalities, athletes, and coaches mourned his death and delivered messages that all pointed to the fact that Wooden inspired them to be who they were at that point. John Wooden would die as college basketball's greatest coach of all time and as one of the most inspirational figures not only in the world of professional sports but also in the realm of success.

Chapter 3: What Made John Wooden a Good Leader?

Seven-Point Creed

Everything about John Wooden's path to success starts with his seven-point creed. This creed was not his original work but was handed down to him by his father Joshua upon his graduation from the eighth grade. Since then, Wooden has lived by this creed and used it on his path to success. Of course, John Wooden would also pass this creed on to his players and everyone who has had the pleasure of working with and under him.

This is John Wooden's seven-point creed:

1. Be true to yourself.
2. Make each day your masterpiece.
3. Help others.
4. Drink deeply from good books, especially the Bible.
5. Make friendship a fine art.

6. Build a shelter against a rainy day.

7. Pray for guidance and give thanks for your blessings every day.

Among the seven creeds that John Wooden lived by, the first one was what always struck him the most. Being true to yourself was one of John Wooden's life mantras. He would first learn about how important this creed was by observing his father Joshua and by seeing how the older Wooden lived his life on an everyday basis.[x]

The young John Wooden would grow up admiring how gentle and caring his father was to all living creatures no matter how small or large they were. He displayed this love when interacting with John's mother. Joshua's often lived by Lincoln's words that say that a father should always love his children's mother. But Joshua's kindness and gentleness were never limited to his interaction with his wife. While living on a farm, John Wooden saw how his father was able to persuade his farm animals, not by forcing them to do work, but by treating them with kindness and gentleness.[ix]

Over time, John Wooden would come to realize that Joshua's kind and gentle nature came from the fact that he was always true to himself. His father was not a wealthy man and was merely a farmer. However, Joshua always brought with him an air of contentment and self-confidence.[ix] He was able to achieve a state of peace by being content with who he was instead of acting like someone he was not.

John Wooden would learn from his father that being kind should never be mistaken for someone's weakness. The fact was that kindness meant that a person was strong enough to take whatever challenge was in front of him. Because of this, Wooden tried to live every day of his life trying his best to be as gentle, kind, content, and confident as his father was. He approached extrapersonal interaction and coaching true to his belief that peace of mind is achieved by being consistent with one's core values. As such, he always saw that being true to one's self was how someone achieves self-confidence as a successful leader.[ix]

The last point of his seven-point creed was also just as influential to John Wooden as any of the other six. Like his father, John Wooden lived by Abraham Lincoln's words. His favorite Lincoln quote was, "If we magnified our blessings the way we magnify our disappointments, we'd all be a lot happier." Simply put, Wooden believed that accepting disappointments was a crucial part of how to be thankful.[xi]

One of the many ways that John Wooden learned that accepting disappointments was a key part of success was through his father, Joshua. When John Wooden was in his early teens, the family lost their farm because of circumstances outside of their control. However, the future Hall of Fame coach never saw his father complain about it or put the blame on another. Instead, Joshua moved on and made the best out of the situation. The same was also true with his mother Roxie, who lost her two daughters at young ages. John Wooden never saw his mother complain or feel bad about the situation. She focused on what was there and then, which was raising John and his brothers.[x]

John Wooden would always emphasize a Chinese saying that says that inner peace is achieved when a person is free from his desires. But at the same time, Wooden would also underscore the importance of cultivating and appreciating the things that a person has instead of comparing what he did not have with others. At the same time, he also preached that one should never take for granted the gifts that were given to him. This included, among other things, life and nature themselves.[x]

By linking thankfulness to his first creed, John Wooden preached the importance of contentment, not only as a means of being true to one's self, but also as a way of making the most out of what a person had. As he often said, contentment makes poor men rich while discontent makes rich men poor. He meant that a person should always be thankful for what he has instead of being discontent with the things he did not have.

Finally, when asked whether he was able to live up to the seven-point creed that his father handed down to him, John Wooden said that he was not what he wanted to be. He was still thankful that he was not the person he was yesterday because of he was trying his best to improve by living up to the creed he lives by, and by never stopping to reach his goals no matter how daunting it might seem.[x]

John Wooden's seven-point creed may not always be consistent with what other people believe in, but there is no denying that his words and beliefs have a sense of universality. When a person becomes content with who he is and what he has, he becomes more confident with himself. And when a person is content and confident, he is thankful for what whatever he has. For Wooden, an effective leader knows who he is and is thankful for what he is.

The Two Sets of Three

A lot of John Wooden's effective leadership comes from how his father handed down principles and philosophies that he lives by. Other than the seven-point creed, Joshua had a twin set of rules he called "The Two Sets of Three." The first set was all about a person's integrity. The second set was about how a person should deal with adversity.[xii]

1. Never Lie. Never Cheat. Never Steal.[xi]

   While all those rules are easy to understand at a glance, there was always something more than what they meant. For John Wooden and his father, the most basic question when it comes to interaction among friends, co-workers, and peers, among others, is if they can trust you. By following those three rules, a person can be known as someone trustworthy to people he comes across.

As a teacher and coach, John Wooden always believed that the best way a person can teach is by setting a good example. It all starts with how he sets himself up as a model of a person that follows a set of rules that he lives by instead of adjusting his code of ethics and beliefs based on the situation he is in or the people who are around him.

Because of this, John Wooden was always considered by his friends, players, and co-workers as a good example of a person striving for success. He always lived a life of integrity and honesty, such as paying for every personal phone call he placed over the school's phones or by taking all of his packages and correspondence to the post office by himself instead of asking someone to do it for him.

And true to being the model of integrity that he is, he would impart words that could help a person live a life of trustworthiness.

"Tell the truth. That way, you don't have to remember a story."

"The true athlete should have character, not be a character."

"Young people need models, not critics."

2. Don't Whine. Don't Complain. Don't Make Excuses.[xiii]

As previously mentioned, the best way that a person could teach is by setting himself up as a good example. As a coach, he is often the reflection of how his team acts. Players would usually absorb the demeanor of their coach and how he acted during times of adversity. A coach that panics and gets frustrated when calls and situations do not go their way would tend to reflect the same attitude to his players, who would also panic and show frustration in similar situations. But if a coach controls his emotions and acts with a cool head amidst the adversity surrounding him, his players would most likely act the same way.

We have often seen successful basketball coaches that have been good examples for their players despite the adversity they face. Phil Jackson is known for not pushing the panic button by calling a timeout whenever his team is on the losing end of a run. Instead, he allows his players to take control of the situation and does not show any panic even though the opposing team has the momentum on their side.

The Golden State Warriors' Steve Kerr, a follower of John Wooden's teachings, always shows the same composure and cool he has in whatever situation his team is with. He rarely shows any kind of frustration even if the situation has not been kind to his team. And because of his carefree nature and poised composure, the Warriors have played with the same kind of demeanor on their way to winning the 2015 and 2017 NBA championships.

Gregg Popovich of the San Antonio Spurs has established a two-decade dynasty by setting himself up as a good example of discipline and composure for his players. He is stoic on the sidelines and never shows any emotion whether his team is up or down by a bunch of points. In turn, the Spurs players that have played under him over the last 20 years show the same kind of demeanor in whatever situation they were in. They always play under control and as relaxed as their head coach.

For John Wooden's part, he saw how to handle adversity through the lenses of his father. It was during the 1920's when the Wooden family lost their farm. Before that, Joshua had purchased pigs that needed a vaccination. It turned out that the vaccine did not work as intended, which led to the deaths of all the pigs he bought on mortgage. And because of a drought that ravaged the crops, the family lost their farm to the bank after missing out on the mortgage payments.

But amidst the adversity that surrounded the Wooden family, Joshua never made any excuses, nor did he whine about the situation they were in. Instead, he looked ahead and moved the family to work as a masseur. John Wooden saw how those events dampened his father's spirit. But despite that, he also realized that his father never dwelled on his broken heart or the misfortune that forced the family off of the farm. This was how John was introduced to how he and others should handle adversity.

John Wooden would go through the same adversity that would have broken the hearts of lesser men or would have had other people make excuses for themselves. When Wooden took the coaching job at UCLA, the basketball team had to share their practice facilities with other teams. They did not even have a home stadium and would have to play in the arenas of other schools. But John Wooden never let the situation hold him back. He would coach the UCLA Bruins to the top of the Pacific Conference though critics had previously doubted that they would perform well.

While John Wooden would not see himself making any success in the NCAA Tournament in his first 12 years as the Bruins' coach, he nevertheless never used UCLA's poor facilities as an excuse. Instead, he broke the habit of complaining by focusing on the team's best assets—their players. Wooden would coach his players all the way to an undefeated season in 1964 even though the odds were against them. This all culminated in the first of his ten NCAA championships.

As Wooden often said, "Things usually turn out the best for people who make the best out of the way things turn out." While John Wooden was never in the best situation concerning facilities and school support when he was yet to become a championship coach for the UCLA Bruins, he used whatever resources he had to formulate a title-worthy system and to make use of his players' skills and talents to bring home the bacon at the end of the NCAA season.

Wooden's Wisdom

John Wooden spent a lifetime imparting wisdom to his players and students. Most of what he preached was the cornerstones of what made him as successful of a coach as he was. And on his part, it also what drove his players and students to strive for the same success that Wooden did in his lifetime. As a teacher, John Wooden loved mentoring people on how to live life to the fullest. His words would become life lessons that would later be called "Woodenisms." These words would play a large part in John Wooden's path to success.[xiv] These are some of John Wooden's most famous Woodenisms:

Be Enthusiastic about your work.

John Wooden was always enthusiastic about his work. He enjoyed his career as a teacher. He spent a lifetime coaching basketball teams and even other sports at one point in his career. And early in his life, he did all of that while playing professional basketball. He never once showed any kind of apathy towards what he did in his life.

Enthusiasm would play a part as one of Wooden's cornerstones in his "Pyramid of Success." He would always say that enthusiasm is what drives a person to perform to the fullest of his abilities and potential. And if a person was not enthusiastic about what he was doing, he was like a machine going through the motions that would not give them the competitive drive to succeed in their endeavors.

Don't get angry when people test you.

John Wooden was always the model of how to handle adversity. Despite all of the odds stacked against him, he rarely showed anger or any hint of frustration. Even the small things never bothered him. However, Wooden would also point out that a lack of anger meant that a person was backing out from fighting for what he believed in. He always preached that a person can fight for his beliefs without getting angry.

One of the more famous stories about Wooden's ability to handle a situation without getting angry was with Bill Walton, one of his most beloved stars in UCLA. Walton once showed up for a pictorial sporting a full beard that would later make him famous in the NBA. This did not sit well with John Wooden, who had a strict policy with how his players wore their hair. But Walton told the coach that he did not have the right to tell him how to wear his hair. True enough, Wooden agreed, but also told Walton that he had the right to decide who was on the team. Fearing that he would lose his spot on the team, Bill Walton showed up to the next practice with his beard shaved.

Don't be afraid to fail.

For John Wooden, failures and disappointments are what makes a person strive for better. His family had its share of failures when they lost the farm when Wooden was still young. However, that did not stop the Wooden family from trying hard to recover from that loss. They were able to recover after moving out of their hometown. And after that, John Wooden was able to forge a respectable career as one of Indiana's brightest young basketball stars.

The lesson that John Wooden would like people to take out of that is that being afraid to fail will hinder a person from doing the things he is capable of. With the constant fear of failure looming over a person's head, he would always ask himself what could have happened had he took the risk instead of listening to what his fears said. And for him, there is no shame in failing if a person did all that he could to prepare himself for success. Failure is just a step toward success. But fear of failure is what hinders a person from taking that fateful step.

Pay attention to the little things.

Bill Walton once shared one of the most memorable moments he had in his time in UCLA and with John Wooden. He remembered that the first thing that John Wooden taught him and the rest of the new players were how to put on their socks and shoes correctly. Wooden always told them that this little part of a basketball player's routine is the initial lesson for everything else they needed to know in the sport.[xv]

When asked why John Wooden put so much emphasis on how to wear socks and shoes correctly, his answer was simple. He said that there is always a danger that your shoes might get untied when you are playing. When that happens, it hinders the flow of the game, and a player may even get injured. And when a player does not wear his socks correctly, there is also the possibility that he might get blisters that would make it uncomfortable to move around.[xiv]

It was this small detail of a person's everyday life that John Wooden paid attention to. While some people might look at wearing socks and putting on their shoes as a routine they would hardly spend extra time on, Wooden believed that paying attention to such a small detail helps a person improve his perspective on the nuances of the game. A large perspective is the sum of all the smaller parts it is composed of. And for John Wooden, every one of those small details matters.

Remember that success is not defined by victories.

The society we live in often teaches us that our victories are what measures our success. In school, our success is measured by how high are grades are. In the professional realm, a person is deemed more successful the more money he earns. In the social world, the more popular the person is, the more successful he is considered by the people around him. And in sports, an athlete's greatness and success are measured by the number of rings he has on his fingers or by the times he has hoisted a championship trophy above his head.

But for John Wooden, success is not best defined by victories. As ironic as it may sound for a ten-time national champion coach, Wooden never once told his players to measure their worth by the titles they won. Instead, what was more important for him was that his players and students were able to make themselves better by striving hard for victories. John Wooden defines success as a person's "peace of mind" that comes from the satisfaction he gets from the fact that he made the exerted the best efforts possible to achieve victory though he might end up failing. John Wooden saw that self-fulfillment was a better measure of success than victories, grades, and money were.

The Pyramid of Success

The foundation of John Wooden's teachings can be found in what he calls his "Pyramid of Success." The history of the pyramid can be traced back to when Wooden first coined his meaning of success. In 1934, Wooden was a high school teacher and basketball coach. It was then and there when he taught his students and players what success meant to him. For Wooden, "success is a peace of mind which is a direct result of self-satisfaction in knowing that you made an effort to do the best of which you are capable of." Since John Wooden never preached that victory was the ultimate measure of success, his philosophy in creating the Pyramid of Success revolved around his definition of the word.

As time passed, John Wooden realized that his definition of success was not enough to help his students and players reach their goals. He thought that they needed something more concrete—a diagram that could help them step by step. Wooden would remember his old high school coach's "Ladder of Achievement," but realized that he needed something more original and something that spoke about him more. This was how he thought of developing the Pyramid of Success, whose structure was inspired by his Wooden's studies about the Great Pyramid of Giza.[xvi]

Wooden knew that all structures should begin with a solid foundation and cornerstones that could withstand hardships, and he would form a strong base for his pyramid. His foundation is composed of industriousness, friendship, loyalty, cooperation, and enthusiasm. And believing that they were both the most important part of his pyramid's foundation, he selected industriousness and enthusiasm as the cornerstones that would support his pathway to success. John Wooden always believed that working hard and being enthusiastic about your work were always some of the most important qualities that a person must have to be successful.

Industriousness

For John Wooden, there is never a substitute for hard work. Success can be achieved first and foremost by working hard for it. No success can ever be achieved unless the person works hard and does it by carefully laying out his plans towards his goals. Rarely do you ready people achieving something worthwhile without having to work hard for it. In all the legends, myths, and epics, all of the successes and great adventures and treasures achieved have been because the hero of the story worked hard. Thus, when traversing the road towards success, one should always start with industriousness.

Friendship

John Wooden always believed that friendship comes from people mutually respecting each other and devoting time to improve each other's self-esteem. He described friendship as something similar to marriage. For a successful marriage to happen, there must be a joint effort between the two parties. The same can be said about friendship, which is what Wooden believes is a good foundation for success. A person will always want to give more to someone he respects and loves. That was why Wooden always sought the friendship of his players and everyone he had to work with. He knew that they were willing to give anything to him if he was willing to do so as well.

Loyalty

Since he never believed in blind loyalty, John Wooden always emphasized that being loyal to one's self is the most critical aspect of the word. However, one must also be loyal to the people depending on him. Success can never be achieved by a one-man team. People should learn to depend on one another to a certain degree. And one way of fostering that mutual interdependence is by being loyal to one another.

Everyone wants to be in an organization with a leader that is loyal to everyone working for and with them. Such a leader would most likely be caring, fair, and considerate because of his loyalty to the people depending on him. And for Wooden, it is something that starts from the top and trickles all the way down to the bottom of the organizational structure.

Cooperation

No man is ever an island. John Wooden always believed that a person should know how to cooperate with everyone in his organizational circle. No matter how high the level of the person is or how low his rank may be, cooperation among co-workers is always necessary. A person must know how to listen to his co-workers if he wants to be heard. For Wooden, this is integral in finding the way that could best benefit everyone involved in the journey to success. As the coach himself would put it, two strong horses cannot pull a carriage if they move in different directions but would be able to carry even the heaviest of loads if they were going the same way.

Enthusiasm

John Wooden believed that a person must enjoy what he is doing because there is no sense of fulfillment in success that the person does not enjoy having. This is why enthusiasm is one of his two cornerstones. A person's heart must be in his work, and everyone around him should have the same mindset. Coupled with industriousness, enthusiasm is considered a vital cog in the machine that drives the entire pyramid to work. Success first comes when a person works hard for what he wants and loves the work he does. That is why, along with industriousness, enthusiasm is one of his cornerstones.

The next layer Wooden's Pyramid of Success is composed of self-control, alertness, initiative, and intentness. Everything on this layer of the pyramid is all about how John Wooden values a person's mental approach above all the physical tools he has. While Wooden wanted his players to be physically quick, it was more important to him that they were mentally sharp. That is why he would often stress to his players that being in a hurry was the worst thing they could do[xvii].

Self-Control

A person needs a great deal of restraint on his way to the top of his goals. What Wooden meant by self-control is a person's ability to avoid temptations, emotionalism, and lack of effort. And for him, self-control was always the sixth man on his team. It was a six on five effort every time on the floor because of how his team had self-control on their side.

Alertness

One of the reasons why John Wooden idolized the great American president Abraham Lincoln was because of his alertness. Lincoln often said that he learns a lesson or two from almost every person he comes across. Wooden loved this characteristic because it gives a person the ability to be able to see the full picture of what was happening around him. Like a driver who will most likely crash if he lacks alertness, an organization would meet the same fate if one of the key pieces of that team is not alert enough to see what is going on around him and to learn a thing or two from what is happening. Alertness is being perceptive.

Initiative

A person who lacks initiative is someone who is doomed to fail. Initiative is what drives the person to act on what they should do. John Wooden always preached that failure is not the scariest part of life. Instead, what a person should fear the most is inaction. There is always some failure when a person acts towards his success. Success is not guaranteed and neither is failure. However, failure is always guaranteed when there is inaction and lack of initiative. That is why Wooden stressed the importance of acting on one's initiative and to be prepared in all cases. This is the reason why he tells his players to never be in a hurry.

Intentness

For John Wooden, intentness means a person's ability to be able to stay focused on the goal and to stay the course even when the voyage may be at its most difficult and challenging parts. It is the ability never to quit and to be persistent and determined no matter the cost. Wooden knew that the path to success will always be long and arduous, but will eventually be worth all the hard work. After all, nothing worth having comes easy.

The third layer of John Wooden's pyramid is what he called "the heart of the body," which is crucial in any structure. Wooden said that architects would often stress the heart of their buildings, and the legendary head coach stressed the importance of three essential characteristics: condition, skill, and team spirit. Those are what he called the heart of his pyramid.

Condition

John Wooden described this as a person's all-around condition. It comprises a person's mental, moral, and physical conditions. That was why he often stressed the importance of a balanced and healthy lifestyle. Wooden preached to his players to rest as often as they could and to follow a healthy diet. Along with that, he also taught that moderation in everything should be followed because too much of something can never be a good thing. And while everyone would always point out how great the UCLA players were concerning conditioning, Wooden was always more proud of how they were in top moral and mental condition. And when it comes to condition, it all starts with making the right choices.

Skill

For John Wooden, skill does not necessarily cover only the person's talents and abilities in a certain field like basketball. It also covers his knowledge about the field and his ability to execute the fundamentals quickly. Some players may have more talent and athleticism than others yet lack the knowledge and execution of fundamentals that players of lesser abilities have. This was why Wooden emphasized the importance of being able to cover every detail when it comes to preparation. This is why skill is at the center of his pyramid. It is the heart of what he believes is the pathway to success. However, a person should always be open to learning. Mastery requires years of continuous study and research. And because of this, John Wooden believes that an effective leader is one that aims to be a lifelong learner.

Team Spirit

Why this characteristic is one of the hearts of John Wooden's Pyramid of Success is simple. For Wooden, a person must always be considerate of others. Organizational success comes from the fact that everyone in the organization has given up on their interests for the benefit of the better good and welfare of everyone involved in the team setup. It is this spirit of unselfish behavior that tends to make people care more about others and the organization as a whole rather than their selfish desires and goals. That was why Wooden always sought players that could fill in the puzzle. A person willing to sacrifice is someone that could make a team great while a person who is not ready to do so is individually great. As for Wooden, he wanted someone that could make the team great instead of someone that had great talent.

As John Wooden's pyramid reaches the top, he has two connecting blocks that relate everything below to what he deems as the apex of success. Those two blocks are poise and confidence, which he thought are both vital when it comes to a person's path to the apex of success. Confidence and poise are what makes a person more competitive. Of course, those two qualities come from the fact that the person is prepared. Poise is necessary for the person to be at ease with himself while confidence comes from preparation and keeping all things in the proper perspective. Those who lack those two essential connecting blocks are often those that fold under pressure when situations get tough.[xvi]

Poise

Being yourself is the first step towards poise. Never pretend to be someone you are not. At the same time, a person who is poised knows how to handle the situation at hand and is never rattled by anything that comes their way. Poise also means that a person holds his values and principles in high regard. No matter what the circumstance may be, a poised person holds true to his beliefs. And for Wooden, those with poise have a brave heart because of how they keep themselves true no matter what happens.

Confidence

For Wooden, confidence is something attained through preparation and excellence. You pursue assets and abilities that make you competent, and that makes a person more confident about himself and the preparations that he has laid down in his path towards success. However, confidence should never be mistaken for arrogance. Arrogance may be the same as confidence at some point, but it is highly destructive and disruptive. Arrogance is the belief that achievements may be repeated without putting in the same hard work and preparation to get to that point in the first place. However, confidence means that a person is still willing to be excellent in his field though he may have already reached the highest level of competency.

Competitive Greatness

The final block of the Pyramid of Success is competitive greatness, which Coach John Wooden described as being at a person's best when it is needed and to enjoy every challenge that faces him. It sits alone at the highest block of the pyramid because Wooden believed that loving the thrill of the competition is what drives the person to love the struggle, the journey, and the fight. He believes that it is a significant building block of success because a competitive person would always be driven to do better when faced with hard challenges. Those tough battles are his best motivators. But competitive greatness is at the top because it cannot be achieved without first having to lay down all of the blocks before it.

When a person achieves all of the building blocks, he will be able to reach the pinnacle of the pyramid, which is the kind of success that Wooden himself defined. Of course, faith and patience are just as important as any other building block. That is why Wooden considers those two aspects as the points that connect the entire set of building blocks to his definition of success.

While John Wooden's leadership excellence all started when his father gave him the Seven-Point Creed, he eventually started to mold leaders of the same caliber with his Pyramid of Success. The pyramid is the omega to the Seven-Point Creed's alpha. Wooden himself became a good leader through the experiences that he went through and from the teachings that he got from his father and all the mentor figures he had in his life. However, through his Pyramid of Success, he became the same kind of mentor that turned ordinary people into similarly successful leaders.

The best thing about John Wooden's leadership and accomplishments was that they were never limited to basketball. Wooden brought together a UCLA community that never had the right love for its basketball program before the legendary head coach arrived. He turned any players' dreams into a reality by leading them to titles and by helping them become champions long after their days at UCLA. And since Wooden's teachings and pyramid almost never had any reference to basketball or coaching, it had become anyone's roadmap and diagram towards success in any field. Businessmen, celebrities, players, and coaches alike have all subscribed to Wooden's beliefs. And more likely than not, they have become successful in the way John Wooden defines the word.

Chapter 4: How John Wooden Maximized Talent

John Wooden was not only an extraordinary coach when it comes to winning basketball games and securing titles for the UCLA Bruins. He was also incredibly talented at bringing the best out of his players. During his time with the Bruins, UCLA was a hot destination for the best prep players that would not only become stars in the collegiate ranks but also in the NBA.

The list of John Wooden's best UCLA products would always start with Kareem Abdul-Jabbar, who was then known as Lew Alcindor. The gigantic 7'2" center was not only tall and big but was also unstoppable under Wooden's tutelage. In the 90 games that he played for UCLA, he would lose just two. And in the three years he played as a Bruin, Abdul-Jabbar would win the NCAA award three times while also getting named the tournament's best player. He was so good under John

Wooden that even the dunk shot was outlawed primarily because of him.

But Kareem did not triumph in college just because of his size. A lot of gigantic players at that time could not win just by using their size alone. Back in the 50's, Wilt Chamberlain went without a national title in college, though he was already considered the most dominant player at that time. Artis Gilmore, the next best center that rocked the NCAA shortly after Abdul-Jabbar went pro, could not win a title primarily because of how much better the Bruins were than his team at that time. While Kareem was a talented center, he might not have been as successful as a winner as he was had he not played for John Wooden. Abdul-Jabbar may have been dominant in college, but he was even better in the NBA. He would win the MVP award and the NBA title six times while also forging a two-decade career that would make him the league's all-time leading scorer.

Closely following Kareem Abdul-Jabbar is Bill Walton. Walton did not have the flair and dominance that Kareem had, but he was a productive center in all facets of the game. Walton was an all-around threat under Wooden's tutelage. He could dominate inside the floor, make plays from both the low and high post, and beat opponents on the strength of his defensive mastery. When he was the main man in the middle for Wooden, Bill Walton won a record of 73 consecutive games as a Bruin. The only smudge to what could have been a perfect tenure as a Bruin was that he was unable to win the national title during his final year of eligibility in college. Walton was not only successful in college but would also win titles and even an MVP when he turned pro.

Sidney Wicks, who was a member of the UCLA Bruins team that won titles from 1969 to 1971, did not initially shine as a player when he was playing behind Abdul-Jabbar in his first year with the team. He was but a role player that did not seem like he was going to be a future star. Nobody even saw the Bruins as legitimate title favorites in 1970 when Kareem had just left the team to go pro. But Wicks exploded to become the best player in a Bruins team that distributed the scoring load after the towering 7'2" Alcindor had left for the NBA. He was even responsible for making life difficult for the much bigger and more dominant center Artis Gilmore back in the 1970 NCAA Finals when UCLA went up against Jacksonville. Wicks was also responsible for bridging the Abdul-Jabbar and Walton eras, which totaled seven titles in all.

While most of John Wooden's best players were big men, Gail Goodrich is arguably the best guard to have ever played under him. Goodrich did not win a title back in 1963, but he was a part of the Bruins team that broke out of UCLA's NCAA slump during his second year under Wooden. It was only in 1964, during Goodrich's breakout year, when the Bruins started winning titles.

Goodrich was one of the primary cogs of the UCLA pressing defense that the press would dub the Bruins Blitz. He was quick when it came to pressuring the ballhandler and was even faster when running for a basket after forcing a turnover. Because of his importance to that 1964 team, the UCLA Bruins went undefeated on its way to giving John Wooden his first NCAA title. Goodrich would help the Bruins win a second title in 1965 to become one of the first UCLA players to win back-to-back national titles.

Keith Wilkes, who would later be called Jamaal, was the Robin to Bill Walton's Batman. He was never the star player for the Bruins under John Wooden, but was a legitimate part of the system that revolved around Walton's ability to make passes from the post. Along with Walton, he would win two titles in 1972 and 1973 while being a part of the team that won 73 straight games. Together with fellow UCLA alum and Wooden product Kareem Abdul-Jabbar in the NBA, he would win titles as a Laker while also playing a crucial role for the 1974-75 Golden State Warriors that won a championship in his rookie season as a pro.

Wrapping up the list of some of the best players to have ever played under John Wooden is Walt Hazzard. He may have only won one title as a Bruin, but Hazzard was the foundation for what would soon become a UCLA dynasty. He was a member of that 1962 team that won an NCAA game and sent the Bruins to the Final Four for the first time under John Wooden. Together with Goodrich, he was an anchor for that pressing backcourt defense. And with him being the primary ballhandler, the Bruins Blitz was at its best with him and Goodrich running the floor after forcing turnovers.

It is no secret that some of basketball's best players had the pleasure of playing and learning under John Wooden when they were in UCLA. However, Wooden was never a coach that placed all his eggs in the basket of one star player. John Wooden was always known for being able to get the most out of his players from top to bottom. For example, the undefeated 1963-64 UCLA Bruins had two other players that averaged double digits in points other than Goodrich and Hazzard. And during Kareem's first season with the Bruins during the 1966-67 season, three other players were helping the soon-to-be all-time great with the scoring load. They were even better the following year when six Bruins, including Abdul-Jabbar, averaged double digits concerning scoring.

When Abdul-Jabbar left the program to go pro, the Bruins were left without a legitimate dominant scorer during the 1969-70 season. But John Wooden was able to get the best out of Sidney Wicks together with other role guys such as John Vallely, Henry Bibby, Curtis Rowe, and Steve Patterson, who were all good players but were never stars. Through their team play and swarming defense, they were able to stop the seemingly unstoppable Artis Gilmore in the title game against Jacksonville in 1970.

But none of John Wooden's teams embodied maximized talent more than the 1975 championship team, which brought the Bruins coach his tenth and final national title before retiring. That title team did not have a legitimate star player. The best players were Dave Meyers and Rich Washington, who would make the NBA but would not become stars as professionals. Wooden maximized the talent of that team so well that he made both Meyers and Washington look like stars. And Marques Jackson, who was still in his first year with the team, showed tremendous potential under John Wooden that season. And with the way they emphasized team play and maximizing each other's potential, they were able to win the Bruins' final NCAA title under John Wooden.

In each of John Wooden's ten titles in 12 years, he has had the luxury of having great talented players. Not only was he able to get the best out of Goodrich, Abdul-Jabbar, Walton, and all the others, but he was also able to turn those players from great players into all-time great leaders. They would take their leadership skills from UCLA all the way to the NBA to become champions. And more often than not, they would credit the roots of their greatness to John Wooden's tutelage when they were still playing for UCLA. But how exactly did Wooden get the most out of his players?

Discipline

"Discipline yourself, and others won't need to."

John Wooden always stressed and emphasized the importance of discipline. But before he got to preach how crucial it was for a person to be disciplined, he first had to discipline himself. Discipline was one of the key lessons that John Wooden got from his father. He lived a life of discipline by spending much of his early morning hours as a child helping out with farm chores and by making sure he had enough time left in the day for his schoolwork.

As a basketball coach, Wooden was so meticulous and disciplined that every detail mattered to him. He was diligent in recording everything he saw on the floor and writing them down on note cards. He was meticulous in his preparation for practices, even going as far back as the last 25 seasons to compare and contrast different sets and plays he records.

John Wooden also emphasized discipline as a critical part of his Pyramid of Success. He elaborated discipline in self-control. Self-discipline was a critical part of how a player could improve his control over his person. Whether it was a physical or mental activity, desirable results can only be obtained by practicing discipline and self-control.

Wooden also stressed how lack of emotion plays a big part in discipline. For him, reason takes a back seat whenever emotions take over a person. And because of that, his actions would not be what he would have desired them to be. He compared this to how parents would discipline their children. John Wooden said that one should never use emotions in disciplining children because that would defeat the purpose of being a positive influence on them. Discipline is never to punish. The goal of it is to correct, influence, improve, and help. And it is through controlling one's emotions that a person becomes a positive influence as far as discipline is concerned.[xviii]

John Wooden practiced disciplining his players in any manner. He would preach the importance of how to put a few extra minutes into correct wearing socks and putting on shoes to prevent blisters and to make sure that the sneakers never came off during a game. He disallowed the use of any profanity in practice or even in games because it showed that the person lacked any control over his emotions and his mind, which leads all the way down to a lack of discipline and control over his body.[xviii] And as far as disciplining one's body was concerned, John Wooden had a strict policy when it came to how a player should wear his hair.

For John Wooden, every little thing mattered when it came to how a person disciplines himself. It all starts with the little things until it becomes a habit for a person to bring himself up with the self-control desired of him. A person's control over his emotions trickles all the way down to how he controls his body. That was why Wooden's teams were all discipline. They did not gamble on plays or lose their control over bad calls and physical plays. He got the most out of his players just by teaching them the importance of self-control and discipline.

Preaching the Fundamentals

John Wooden drilled into the minds of all the players that have played for him the importance of fundamentals. What Wooden considered the necessary skills of a basketball player to be dribbling, shooting, rebounding, passing, and defending. All five of those fundamentals were what he found to be the most crucial skills that a player should have.

Every day at practice, Wooden had all of his players practice the fundamentals no matter how big or small they were. Everyone learned how to dribble, shoot, rebound, pass, and defend regardless of what position they were asked to play. He thought that everybody should focus on the fundamentals that a basketball player needed to have instead of on the flair and showmanship that had enveloped the game through the NBA.

If there was anything that John Wooden hated about basketball, it was that it had become a showcase instead of a sport that focused on the players' fundamentals. Basketball was slowly becoming more about a player's ability to entertain with dunks, long-range shots, acrobatic layups, and spectacular statistical performances. This was the reason why he discouraged his players from watching the NBA, especially the Los Angeles Lakers, their local professional basketball team.[xix]

Back when John Wooden was coaching the Bruins, the Los Angeles Lakers had some of the greatest names in basketball history. They had incredible showmen such as Wilt Chamberlain, Jerry West, and Elgin Baylor, who could all put on a show with spectacular moves, dunks, and shots that nobody in the world had ever seen. Even Gail Goodrich, a former Bruin under Wooden, had gotten himself infected with Laker fever.

As talented and enjoyable to watch as the Los Angeles Lakers were during that era, John Wooden never liked it when his players watched their games. He thought that they would pick up bad habits that were not enjoyable to watch but were unnecessary for the college game. As much as Wooden respected and admired the talented players that the Lakers fielded, he thought that the NBA and the collegiate leagues played a different style.[xix]

With all of his emphasis on how critical it was for players to master the basic skills, John Wooden had also grown to dislike how today's players are allowed to leave college after one year to try their hand at the professional leagues. In an age where dunks, athleticism, three-point shooting, and ball-handling wizardry are more important than the basics of the game, developing the fundamentals while in college has taken a backseat. Nevertheless, John Wooden has always been an advocate of how players do old-fashioned things and how some teams in the college ranks win titles with fundamentally-sound upperclassmen.[xix]

Above all the fundamentals that he thought were vital, John Wooden stressed the importance of conditioning. Good conditioning was not a fundamental basketball skill but was instead a trait that every athlete should have. Conditioning was so crucial for Wooden that it became a building block of his Pyramid of Success.

For him, conditioning was never only about how players were in top physical shape. Wooden thought that it was more important for them to be mentally and emotionally conditioned. The body can only do so much that the mind tells it to do, and for John Wooden, having the player condition his mind and emotions is one way for him to be able to have mastery over his physical conditioning.

And because of how John Wooden emphasized the importance of the basics and good conditioning, his players are some of the most fundamentally sound in the game of basketball. Kareem Abdul-Jabbar made a long and productive NBA career out of the fundamental skills that he learned to hone. Because of his fundamentals, he was able to play until the age of 41 in a 20-year career that saw him compiling the most career points the NBA has ever seen. And Bill Walton, who would have probably been considered one of the all-time greatest players had injuries not slowed him down, became an MVP and a champion with his fundamental skills such as passing, rebounding, and defending. He was always described as probably the most fundamentally sound center in the history of the NBA. It was because of how John Wooden tried his best to get his point across that those players, among others, were able to become two of the most fundamentally sound players that the sport has ever seen.

It may not be popular, but some of today's best NBA teams have been built on the basic skills of their players. Gregg Popovich of the San Antonio Spurs has always stressed the importance of fundamentals over athleticism and individual skill level. In the two decades that he has coached the Spurs, Popovich's teams were all about fundamentals. All of the players knew all the plays and were interchangeable because of how well they could dribble, pass, shoot, defend, and rebound. His emphasis on the basics has yielded him five championship trophies.

The Golden State Warriors under Steve Kerr is a team that has become a marriage between today's emphasis on showmanship and yesteryear's love for the fundamentals. Everyone on that team could do all of the basic skills of a basketball player. They love moving the ball around to find an open shot. They gang rebounded and played the defensive end of the floor at an elite level. And they do all of that while being able to entertain the crowd with their hot three-point shooting and display of ball-handling wizardry. John Wooden could not live long enough to see how Kerr's team was able to combine two different eras. Had he been able to watch them, he would have found the Warriors to be as entertaining as they are fundamental.

Team Play

When asked about the modern-day version of basketball, John Wooden thought that it suffered too much from individual play.[xx] Players were no longer moving the ball the same way they did back in his time. It focused heavily on how an individual player could break a team down and let the other players on the team play off of his skills.

Players such as Michael Jordan and Kobe Bryant have both made all-time great careers on the strength of their ability to play the individual game at the highest level. With their transcendent one-on-one skills, they both thrive as isolation players that allow their teammates to play off them if ever they could not secure baskets.

And while players such as Magic Johnson, LeBron James, and James Harden among others distribute the ball well, they are most effective when they have the ball in their hands to create either for themselves or others. They were players that did not move the ball around but would rather have possession of it until a teammate gets himself open for the best possible shot.

It was those kinds of individual plays that John Wooden thought made the game of basketball suffer. There was too much focus on the individual star instead of having the ball move around until a shot unfolded. Wooden never liked it when the ball was stationary. Instead, he loved the idea of team play by passing the ball around to find the best possible shot rather than giving it to a star player out on the perimeter for isolation plays or to an unstoppable post player that stopped the ball movement whenever he got it near the basket.

It was always important for John Wooden that his players let go of their individual desires for their team play to grow. That is why Team Spirit is one of the hearts of his Pyramid of Success. For Wooden, a team can never prosper when one of the members focuses more on his individual goals rather than sacrificing his desires for the sake of the team.

Back in the day, a lot of doubters and naysayers would rather give more of the credit for UCLA's victories to superstar players Kareem Abdul-Jabbar and Bill Walton, who are arguably the best college basketball players of all time. There were always references to how great and dominant those players were to the point that they were unstoppable no matter what the opposing teams did. Some would say that they were the reason why John Wooden had five more titles under his belt.

But if that were the case, then why could the other teams not do it? Ohio State had a great tandem of Jerry Lucas and John Havlicek from 1959 up to 1962 but did not have the same success as the UCLA Bruins had with their star players. Even Wilt Chamberlain, who is arguably the most dominant basketball player to have ever played in both the college and the pro levels, could not lead Kansas to the Promised Land on the strength of his unstoppable play. Cincinnati never won a national title under Oscar Robertson, who averaged 34 points and 15 rebounds during his three-year stay with the team during the late 50's. And even Pete Maravich, who would go down as the NCAA's all-time leading scorer after averaging 44 points in the three years, could not secure a title for LSU from 1967 to 1970.

The answer is that basketball was never about team play, and the UCLA Bruins were never just about how great Abdul-Jabbar and Walton were. John Wooden said that the Bruins might not have won their titles had Kareem and Bill decided to take the selfish route. Instead, they both decided to give their all to the team and did what the coach asked them to do because winning was on their minds.[xxi]

And when the stars were doing their best to be unselfish and to do whatever the coach asked them to do, it became a lot easier for all the other guys to do the same. One of John Wooden's favorite players was Swen Nater. He would call Nater one of the greatest players to have ever played for him, but not because of his on-court impact or talent. He was merely Bill Walton's backup. However, what made him great in the eyes of Wooden was that he was unselfish and willing to do what the coach wanted him to do.[xxii]

At 6'11", Swen Nater was comparable to Walton in size. Because of that, Wooden often asked him to make life difficult for Walton during practices. Nater did just that and allowed Bill Walton to improve because of how much his backup was making life difficult for him. And when Nater was on the floor to spell minutes for Walton, he was excellent at securing rebounds and defending the paint in whatever limited time he had. That kind of an unselfish quality and the ability to give his coach what he wanted was what made Nater one of the greatest Bruins as far as Wooden was concerned.

Like John Wooden often stressed, team play is all about forgetting about your individual goals to make the team better. It was not only about simple ball movement or sharing but was more about doing what was necessary to improve the team's performance.

Whether it was being an excellent practice player like Swen Nater or a dominant inside presence like Kareem Abdul-Jabbar, Wooden's definition of what team play is revolves around an unselfish mindset and the desire to do what was needed to secure the win. And through this team play, everyone within the system was able to maximize his talent. Just ask Nater, who went all the way from a backup center to become a leading rebounder in both the ABA and the NBA.

Building Character

The best way that John Wooden maximized his players' talents was not through basketball drills or on-court strategies or systems. It was more about bringing the best out of their characters and to make them better people that could benefit the entire team setup. As Bill Walton once said, John Wooden preached to his players that becoming a good person meant that you have what it takes to become a good basketball player. It was character over talent and skill for Wooden.

John Wooden has always stressed the point that character is the solid foundation of a structure. In a person, character is the foundation of his being. This means that the stronger a person's character is, the better the foundation he has to build his skills and to maximize his potential in whatever endeavor he might seek in life. Character always matters because it is what breaks or makes a man.

Bill Walton summed it up best when he described how John Wooden influenced his character. He said that Wooden never emphasized the importance of winning but would rather talk about the effort it takes to win. He rarely talked about basketball but enjoyed discussing life. And best of all, he rarely talked about strategies, plays, or systems. He would rather talk about the best people and the character that it took to get them to where they were.

In his talk during Wooden's memorial, Kareem Abdul-Jabbar said that his coach was all about life's wisdom rather than basketball's statistics and plays. He was so genuinely caring about his players' wellbeing that he was often called a father figure and mentor instead of a coach. He was always the type of person that preached more about character rather than basketball. After all, his Pyramid was never about the sport but about how a person gets through life in general as a successful person. And for Kareem, he always thought that Wooden used sports as a way of teaching how to apply themselves to any kind of situation.

Of course, the best way that John Wooden improved his players' character was by being an example himself. Abdul-Jabbar once said that Wooden never asked from his players what he could not ask from himself. He always set himself as the example for his players to follow instead of telling them to be a person they could not concretely see. He became the perfect role model for competitive greatness and how to learn.

Gail Goodrich described the coach as incorruptible. One of the best character lessons that Goodrich learned from Wooden was that a successful winning team can be built without having to sacrifice personal beliefs and without breaking any values. While Goodrich initially thought that Wooden was teaching him basketball, he would realize that what he learned was about life and how to become a better person. And as we know, Goodrich would later become a champion and multiple-time All-Star because of how John Wooden helped him build his character to succeed.

Outside of the X's and O's, the fundamentals, and the ability to play within the team setup, what mattered most for John Wooden was a person's character. Since he considered it the foundation of a person's life, character would ultimately test whether a person was built for success or not. And as a mentor, teacher, and coach, John Wooden's job was not to instill the basics of basketball or the strategic side of the game. His job was to make sure his players' foundation was solid. His job was to help them build their character to prepare them for success. His job was to prepare his players for life. And when all of that falls into place, the player has all the opportunity to maximize his talents as Wooden once said that a good person has a strong chance of becoming a great basketball player.

Chapter 5: The John Wooden System

Defense

It is a familiar adage in basketball and probably in every competitive sport that defense wins championships. Most teams and athletes focus more on offense than defense when it comes to securing titles in their respective sports. The 60's Boston Celtics dominated the era on the strength of Bill Russell's strong defensive play. The 90's Chicago Bulls were known more as a great defensive team rather than an offensive squad that relied on Michael Jordan. Even boxing's Muhammad Ali and Floyd Mayweather are considered two of the greatest of all time because of their unbeatable defensive tactics. The same was true for John Wooden's championship teams.

Before John Wooden's first championship run in 1964, the UCLA Bruins' defense relied primarily on their full-court man-to-man press. All of UCLA's perimeter players would pressure their opponents' ball-handler the moment they tried to cross the halfcourt line. And if the primary ball-handler attempted to make a pass to relieve the pressure off him, a secondary or a third defender would pressure the receiver before he even got the ball to force a steal or turnover.

The UCLA Bruins' full-court man-to-man press defense was what they used to push the tempo up. They would force a lot of turnovers from their opponents to try to increase their possessions and scoring opportunities. The defense would see its pinnacle during the 1962 NCAA Tournament when John Wooden would lead the Bruins all the way to the Final Four.

But during the 1962-63 conference title game against Stanford, John Wooden saw his defense in a different light. They would beat Stanford in a low-scoring game of 51-45. As effective of a defense as they played, the Bruins could not maximize the possessions and tempo as much as they wanted to. They forced 20 turnovers that game but could only score 51 points. This led Wooden to ponder why.

The Bruins would lose to Arizona in the first round of that year's NCAA Tournament. This was when John Wooden realized that changes needed to happen. One of his assistants told him that a full-court man-to-man defensive effort was not enough to push the tempo because it forced the opposing offense to beat the pressure by advancing the ball past the halfcourt line with the dribble. When opponents tried to break the press by advancing the ball, a lot of time gets eaten up. This would eventually lead to fewer possessions on the part of the Bruins, who wanted to maximize the pace of the game for more scoring opportunities.

One of John Wooden's assistants would convince him that the full-court man-to-man was not the most effective defensive style. Instead, he proposed that the Bruins "send gas to a game's engine" by using a full-court zone press. The zone press uses two-man traps against the ball-handler in the backcourt, which forces him to make a pass to advance the ball past the halfcourt line. And with the relative inexperience and lower basketball IQ that young college players had, they would most likely try to break the press by throwing long lobs or cross-court passes that were easy targets for the Bruins' quick hands and feet.[viii] The pass saves more time than the dribble. And when the Bruins pick off those passes with a lot of time left on the clock, they would have more opportunities to score because of the increased tempo.

Because of the turnovers caused by UCLA's long arms and quick feet, the Bruins would score in a hurry. They would do it so suddenly and in bunches that the runs caused by the defense would earn the nickname "Bruin

Blitzes." But for John Wooden, he would say that his team's defense was causing their opponents disharmony and disunity.[viii] John Wooden's 1964 team would eventually win the NCAA Championship with an undefeated run. And before he knew it, it was what led the UCLA Bruins to nine more championships under John Wooden's guidance.

What was beautiful about John Wooden's zone press was that it was a strategy that could live without a dominant big man defending the paint. During the 50's, San Francisco thrived defensively under Bill Russell's defensive genius inside the paint. Meanwhile, an athletic freak of a guard like Oscar Robertson of Cincinnati could force turnovers and defensive plays all by himself because of his sheer size and athleticism. [xxiii]

But John Wooden's earlier championship teams and those squads that did not feature either Kareem Abdul-Jabbar or Bill Walton did not have a large frontline nor did they have superstar players that could lead the defensive charge. Instead, the pre-Kareem days had small guards such as Gail Goodrich and Walt Hazzard manning the backcourt defense. Meanwhile, the front line was composed of 6'5" players such as Keith Erickson and Fred Slaughter, who were both undersized compared to their opponents' big men.

But the beauty of that team was that all of those players were well-conditioned and athletic. John Wooden was a coach that always stressed the importance of conditioning. All of his players were in top shape and could run the pressing defense for hours. Everyone in the backcourt was willing to trap the ball-handler all night long. Meanwhile, Wooden's undersized but athletic frontcourt players were always more than willing to run for the interceptions when the opposing players made errant passes.

As deadly as the zone press was, John Wooden admitted that it had weaknesses. The problem with the zone press comes when the opposing offense breaks it and nobody is back in time to protect the basket. However, Wooden was able to remedy that weakness by having his players run back to play man-to-man the moment the ball crossed the halfcourt line. And with how Wooden's previous teams stressed full-court man-to-man defense, the Bruins were already familiar with how to quickly come back to play honest defense in case their zone press got broken.

Pete Newell of California stated that the press was an integral part of a winning college basketball team because of how it destroys the opposing team's plans. A conventional defensive play reads the offense and reacts according to what happens. However, a pressing defense reverses the status quo by having the offense adjust to how the defensive players pressures and traps the ball-handler. That was how effective the UCLA press was.

John Wooden's press, whether it was full-court, 2-2-1, or 3-1-1, was always effective in making their opponents guess where the trap was coming from and who was coming in to try to pick off the errant pass. UCLA's pressing defense never allowed the opposing offense to dictate the tempo. Instead, they always made sure that the game was quick and that their opponents were wondering what would happen next.

While John Wooden would find himself eventually adjusting his defensive tactics especially during the years when Abdul-Jabbar and Walton were running the team's frontline, the defensive standard was their zone pressing defense. That was how Wooden was able to maximize possessions and force turnovers. And when the press failed, he always had two all-time greats like Kareem and Bill manning the paint. But in the five other championships seasons he had in UCLA, John Wooden utilized the zone press to make up for the team's lack of size and to, of course, fuel their offensive runs.

Offense

What was special about John Wooden's teams was that the offense was most likely a result of how ferociously they played on the defensive end. While using the full-court and zone presses to their advantage, the UCLA Bruins forced turnovers by the bunches and converted them at the other end for quick baskets. And because John Wooden loved stressing the quick-paced game, UCLA was always one of the best teams concerning offense on top of how dominant they were on the defensive end.

Because of the pressing defense that the UCLA Bruins played, John Wooden was able to lead his teams back from huge deficits or close games. It did not matter how big the opposing team's lead was or how close the game was because once the Bruins were able to get in their best defensive zone, they could destroy a deficit or build huge leads in a matter of a few minutes. These Bruins Blitzes were the most feared offensive attacks during John Wooden's tenure as UCLA's head coach.

As John Wooden would describe it when he first implemented the zone press in 1964, his guards Walt Hazzard and Gail Goodrich almost never called plays for the team.[viii] They just let the defense dictate their offensive attack. And when they were able to force turnovers, the Bruins were at their best when they were running and sharing the ball before the opposing defense got set.

John Wooden was described as a coach and visionary ahead of his time. Back then, a lot of teams in the collegiate ranks preferred playing slow-paced styles. They relied on grinding the pace down by playing good halfcourt defense predicated on the defensive abilities of the big men that protected the paint. It was an era when college coaches emphasized how important size was compared to speed.

However, John Wooden was different. Similar to his style when he was still a player, Wooden loved quickening up the pace. He never focused on the factors that he could not control such as size. Instead, he maximized talent by focusing on whatever assets they had. And when Wooden first won a title in 1964, his team never had size. Their tallest player was a backup center that stood 6'7". Their starting center, Fred Slaughter, was 6'5". Instead of dwelling on their lack of size, he made use of how quick and athletic the team was by running them to the ground during practices to improve his players' conditioning and to make them get used to the running style of basketball.[xxiv]

After that 1964 NCAA Championship win, John Wooden would be blessed to coach two of the best centers in college basketball history. He had Kareem Abdul-Jabbar during the latter parts of the 1960's, and from 1972 to 1974, he had Bill Walton. Since both centers stood at least or almost seven feet tall, John Wooden had to adjust his fast-paced offense to accommodate those players' talents.

When it came down to the halfcourt offensive set, John Wooden was one of the first proponents of a game that focused on an attack that relied on a faster pace, more floor spacing, and ball movement. He always liked stressing the importance of ball movement instead of plays that relied on a star players' skills. This was the reason why most of his championship teams had at least five players scoring in double digits.

When Wooden had Abdul-Jabbar, he loved playing a high-low offense that was anchored on how Kareem was so dominant inside the paint. The beauty of his post offense was that it was able to make use of how unstoppable his centers were near the basket while making sure they were able to avoid getting doubled or tripled because of how good the spacing and ball movement was.

Wooden's high-low play relies on how the guards keep the defensive guessing and adjusting by moving the ball around the perimeter. A frontcourt player then positions himself at the high post where he becomes the anchor that either finds an open player on the opposite side of the perimeter or passes down to a big man that ducks into the lane for a post play. This was especially effective when he had Kareem Abdul-Jabbar, and to some extent, Bill Walton

While Walton himself was just as good as Kareem was inside the paint, he was even better as a passer. John Wooden often used Bill Walton as the anchor of his high-post offense. The offense starts with the guards passing the ball to each other while the post player moves from the low to high post. Once the ball gets to the big man near the high post, the two other frontline players would cut towards the basket while the guards position themselves at the perimeter to give the high post man a bunch of choices for the pass. And because of how talented Bill Walton was as a big man passer, he was one of the vital cogs that ran the UCLA offense during the 70's.

In almost any offensive system, both Abdul-Jabbar and Walton would have dominated the possessions and scoring opportunities. They would have probably averaged 30 a night. But for John Wooden, what was important to a championship team was the emphasis on ball movement and unselfishness. It was how he preached teamwork and the importance of sharing possessions that made the UCLA Bruins one of the most feared teams, not only on the defensive end but also on the offensive side of the court as well. It was this mindset that made Kareem, Bill, and all of the other UCLA Bruins that have played under Wooden successful champions in whatever endeavor they chased after learning from the Wizard of Westwood.

Chapter 6: Key Takeaways

The Pyramid of Success

John Wooden's life lessons and secrets to his accomplishments can be found in his Pyramid of Success. He almost never discussed basketball when he wrote about and expanded his pyramid because the focus, for him, was not merely constrained to sports but every other endeavor. It can apply to the realm of business and leadership as well as media and showbiz.

John Wooden describes success as the peace of mind which is a direct result of self-satisfaction in knowing you did your best to become the best you are capable of. Therefore, his Pyramid of Success never discussed how to win or how to be able to triumph over other people. Instead, what was critical to him was that the person poured all of his efforts and hard work into trying to reach his pinnacle of success rather than trying to become successful in the conventional sense of the word.

While effort and love for your work may be the cornerstones of John Wooden's pyramid, he always stressed the importance of the other building blocks that include self-control, team spirit, confidence, and competitive greatness when the person seeks his success. And helping to bridge his building blocks and success, a devout and disciplined man such as John Wooden always placed a lot of importance on faith and patience when it comes to a person's path towards success.

John Wooden would call the Pyramid of Success the fundamental qualities that a person needed in life. Similar to how he coached his teams, Wooden always emphasized how important it was to stick to the fundamentals. And in life, it was just as crucial to stick to the basic skills and qualities that were important. That is why there is nothing new, unique, or novel about Wooden's building blocks. They are all fundamental characteristics and lessons that a person needed to embrace. And on Wooden's part, he simply needed a pyramid, or a diagram, to preach to his students and his players how he defined success.

Throughout the years, John Wooden's success and his pyramid have transcended the world of basketball. Actor Matthew McConaughy once played the role of Coach Dale Brown, who was a Wooden follower, and consulted the Wizard of Westwood himself to learn a great deal about life. NFL quarterback Drew Brees was an awardee of the Wooden Citizenship Cup and often stressed to his family and teammates the importance of John Wooden's teachings and lessons. And Microsoft's Bill Gates himself once invited Wooden as a speaker to his employees and often called the UCLA legend one of the most vital mentors in world history.

Although John Wooden's influence and lessons may have gone beyond sports, his memory will forever be among the most remembered in basketball. Among his players, probably no other UCLA legend has talked about him in such high regard as Bill Walton has.

Walton has called Wooden the single greatest mentor he has had in his life. He even dedicates a shrine in his home to his former UCLA coach. And because of how important to his life John Wooden was, he often preached the lessons that he learned from the legendary coach to his children. And he would even bring them to Wooden himself, who would go on to teach the younger Walton kids same philosophies and lessons that he taught Bill Walton.

Bill Walton would pass down what he has learned from Wooden to his son Luke Walton, who was often called the consummate teammate because of his fundamental skills, leadership capabilities, and unselfish demeanor. Luke would play professional basketball for ten seasons and would win two titles as a Laker. He would go on to win another title as Steve Kerr's assistant with the Golden State Warriors. Kerr himself is also an avid follower of Wooden. And when it is all summed up, the championships and leadership success that Bill Walton, Luke Walton, and Steve Kerr have accomplished in the world of basketball can be traced back to how they all saw John Wooden as one of their life mentors.

An Offense Built on Defense

One of the highlights of John Wooden's coaching career was that first NCAA title he won back in 1964 when he led the UCLA Bruins to an undefeated season by focusing on building an offense based on defense. Since he was described as a coach far ahead of his time, John Wooden stressed the importance of pushing the tempo of the game. It was through the zone press that he was able to maximize possessions to improve the pace of the game.

John Wooden once said that quickness instead of size and speed was the key. His team's quickness on the defensive end and their conditioning the entire game was what was the key to their pressing defense. What the team lacked in size and speed, they made up for in their mental and physical quickness when it came to pressuring their opponents into turnovers and submission.

By forcing turnovers early, John Wooden's teams were built to run and capitalize on their opponents' mistakes to unleash scoring runs that would be affectionately called the Bruins Blitzes. This all started with that undersized but quick 1964 UCLA Bruins team that could not be defeated because of how they used their defense to make offensive runs. Offensive strategies and plays may have changed as his personnel came and went but John Wooden's core principles of using defense as one of the fuels for his offense remained one of the constants in his ten championship squads.

Freedom and Unselfishness

Though Bill Walton may have exaggerated a bit, he described his time under John Wooden as full of freedom. He said that the team was so well-structured and tailored that Wooden never almost needed to use the clipboard to call plays. John Wooden allowed his players to play within the flow of the game using the principles of spacing and ball movement that he always preached during practices. As Walton would put it, Wooden never held his players back from utilizing their talents in an offensive system that allowed them to be free.[xxiv]

On top of making sure that his players played with a lot of freedom and fluidity, John Wooden stressed that success was better achieved through team basketball and ball movement. Most of Wooden's plays and tactics were drawn in such a way that there was almost no opportunity for isolation or hero basketball. He always made sure that everyone had an opportunity to contribute to their cause.

Because of how much he emphasized ball movement, John Wooden never loved how the generations that come after him played isolation and individual ball more often than they should have. Wooden had the pleasure of being able to see stars such as Michael

Jordan, Magic Johnson, Kobe Bryant, Shaquille O'Neal, and LeBron James succeed in the professional basketball ranks. But as good and transcendent as those players were in skills, they were more effective when the ball was in their hands rather than when it was moving around the floor to find the best shots available. As Wooden pointed out, this was one of the things that he thought contemporary basketball was suffering from.

But as standards, offenses, and defenses evolved, teams in the NBA and college ranks have gone back to focusing more on a fast tempo and ball movement rather than on isolation and individual plays. Successful teams have been moving the ball around much more than they have been the past ten years and have also been playing a pace nearly as quick as the NBA once did during the 60's. The emphasis now has been all about pace and space and ball and player movement similar to what John Wooden was preaching to his teams back then. This, and many other things, was one of the reasons Wooden was described as a coach well ahead of his time.

In many ways, the way John Wooden coached his teams' offense is similar to today's modern-day style of basketball. While there was no three-point shot back in Wooden's time, his system mirrors how today's championship teams stress the importance of a fast-paced style that allows players a certain sense of freedom because of all the spacing and the ball movement involved. Golden State Warriors head coach Steve Kerr himself, who grew up in the shadow of Wooden when his father was a professor in UCLA back in the 70's, admitted that the Wizard of Westwood was one of his biggest coaching influences. And when you look at how today's offenses are being played, it is not difficult to say that Kerr was not the only coach that studied how smooth Wooden's offenses ran.

Conclusion

There is almost no argument about John Wooden's standing as college basketball's greatest head coach of all time. It is not even close. He dominated with ten championships in only 12 years during the 60's and 70's. At one point, he even won seven straight titles while no other coach in college basketball history has ever won more than three straight. And trailing behind his ten NCAA titles is Duke's Mike Krzyzewski with only half of that number. Based on those stats alone, it is difficult to argue against Wooden's reputation as the best coach in college basketball history.

However, what made Wooden the greatest of all time in his field was not his title wins. As a coach, he never stressed the importance of winning. What was important to him, according to his definition of success, was that the person was in a state of contentment knowing that he did his best to become his best. Instead, what made John Wooden into a larger-than-life figure not only in the world of college basketball coaching but the entire history of success and leadership was that his lessons transcended beyond sports.

Immortalized in his Pyramid of Success, the lessons and philosophies that John Wooden loved imparting and teaching to students, players, and peers were always more than just about basketball or even competitive sports for that matter. Wooden was not a basketball coach. He was a life mentor. He taught everyone the lessons of how to live their life to the fullest and how to succeed in any chosen endeavor. He was an inspirational figure that turned boys into men, men into leaders, and leaders into mentors. John Wooden was a man that knew how to live and was willing to teach the world the best way he knew how.

All of John Wooden's teachings were visible in almost every aspect of life he tried his hand in. When he was a young boy, he was a hard worker that did not give up despite the difficulties life had to offer. As a young player, he rose to become one of the best basketball players in the state of Indiana but chose to teach and coach rather than to pursue a full-time professional career because of how much he wanted to see other people grow. And as a teacher and a coach, he was at his best.

In the endeavor he pursued until his retirement in 1975, John Wooden touched and inspired students and players to not only do their best as basketball players but also as human beings. Those who have had the pleasure to work with him have become successful individuals. His best players turned into NBA champions and MVP's. His assistants and other players became coaches. And those that have come to admire him from afar through his teachings and writings have also become just as successful in life as he has simply because they did not allow the conventional definition of success to confine them. They instead allowed themselves to be successful by rethinking the meaning of success and made themselves believe that through the building blocks of Wooden's pyramid, they could succeed in the best way they could.

It was how John Wooden transcended college basketball that made him as great as he is to the eyes of not only basketball coaches and players but people from other fields as well. Some would even go on to say that he may even be the best coach not only in college basketball or even against the NBA's coaches but also in all of professional sports because of what he meant, not only to the world of competitive sports, but to life itself as well.

And with John Wooden's name and teachings immortalized in the Basketball Hall of Fame, in his writings, and in the people he has inspired and taught, the world has become an even better place for the nurturing of successful people. Nobody in basketball has ever had the same impact as he had on the sport and to life in general. And perhaps nobody will ever

Final Word/About the Author

I was born and raised in Norwalk, Connecticut. Growing up, I could often be found spending many nights watching basketball, soccer, and football matches with my father in the family living room. I love sports and everything that sports can embody. I believe that sports are one of most genuine forms of competition, heart, and determination. I write my works to learn more about influential athletes and coaches in the hopes that from my writing, you the reader can walk away inspired to put in an equal if not greater amount of hard work and perseverance to pursue your goals. If you enjoyed *John Wooden: The Inspiring Life and Leadership Lessons of One of Basketball's Greatest Coaches,* please leave a review! Also, you can read my works on other coaches such as *Gregg Popovich, Brad Stevens, Erik Spoelstra, Steve Kerr,* and *Doc Rivers.* If you prefer reading biographies on athletes, I have books on *Roger Federer, Novak Djokovic, Andrew Luck, Rob*

Gronkowski, Brett Favre, Calvin Johnson, Drew Brees, J.J. Watt, Colin Kaepernick, Aaron Rodgers, Peyton Manning, Tom Brady, Russell Wilson, Michael Jordan, LeBron James, Kyrie Irving, Klay Thompson, Stephen Curry, Kevin Durant, Russell Westbrook, Anthony Davis, Chris Paul, Blake Griffin, Kobe Bryant, Joakim Noah, Scottie Pippen, Carmelo Anthony, Kevin Love, Grant Hill, Tracy McGrady, Vince Carter, Patrick Ewing, Karl Malone, Tony Parker, Allen Iverson, Hakeem Olajuwon, Reggie Miller, Michael Carter-Williams, John Wall, James Harden, Tim Duncan, Steve Nash, Draymond Green, Kawhi Leonard, Dwyane Wade, Ray Allen, Pau Gasol, Dirk Nowitzki, Jimmy Butler, Paul Pierce, Manu Ginobili, Pete Maravich, Larry Bird, Kyle Lowry, Jason Kidd, David Robinson, LaMarcus Aldridge, Derrick Rose, Paul George, Kevin Garnett, Chris Paul, Marc Gasol, Yao Ming, Al Horford, Amar'e Stoudemire, DeMar DeRozan, Isaiah Thomas, Kemba Walker and Chris Bosh in the Kindle Store. If you love basketball, check out my website at claytongeoffreys.com to join my exclusive list where I let you know about my latest books and give you lots of goodies.

Like what you read? Please leave a review!

I write because I love sharing the stories of influential coaches like John Wooden with fantastic readers like you. My readers inspire me to write more so please do not hesitate to let me know what you thought by leaving a review! If you love basketball, or productivity, check out my website at claytongeoffreys.com to join my exclusive list where I let you know about my latest books. Aside from being the first to hear about my latest releases, you can also download a free copy of *33 Life Lessons: Success Principles, Career Advice & Habits of Successful People*. See you there!

Clayton

References

[i] "John Wooden". *Academy of Achievement*. Web.

[ii] *The Wooden Effect*. Web.

[iii] Ksander, Yael. "Hoosier Hysteria". *Indiana Public Media*. 13 March 2006. Web.

[iv] "John Wooden: A Coaching Legend". *UCLA Basketball*. Web.

[v] Hornsby, Donald. "John Wooden: A Lifetime Masterpiece". *Vision*. 2010. Web.

[vi] Meyer, Paula. "March Madness Flashback: John Wooden". *Indiana State University*. 30 March 2006. Web.

[vii] Purna, Mike. "The Wizard of Westwood". *ESPN*. Web.

[viii] Wolff, Alexander. "Something special about the first: How '64 Bruins made John Wooden". *Sports Illustrated*. 5 June 2010. Web.

[ix] *Wooden Award*. Web.

[x] Impelman, Craig. "John Wooden's 7-Point Creed: 'Be True to Yourself'". *Success*. 13 December 2016. Web.

[xi] Impelman, Craig. "John Wooden's 7-Point Creed: 'Be Thankful'". *Success*. 22 February 2017. Web.

[xii] Impelman, Craig. "Never Lie. Never Cheat. Never Steal.". *The Wooden Effect*. 15 November 2016. Web.

[xiii] Impelman, Craig. "How to Handle Adversity: Don't Whine, Don't Complain, Don't Make Excuses.". *The Wooden Effect*. 29 November 2016. Web.

[xiv] Fisher, Brenna. "Words of Wisdom: UCLA Legend John Wooden". *Success*. 30 June 2008. Web.

[xv] Luther, Claudia. "Coach John Wooden's lesson on shoes and socks". *UCLA Newsroom*. 4 June 2010. Web.

[xvi] Impelman, Craig. " How Coach Wooden Created the Pyramid of Success". *Success*. 15 March 2017. Web.

[xvii] " The Philosophy Behind Coach John Wooden's Pyramid of Success ". *Hub Pages*. 3 July 2014. Web.

[xviii] Impelman, Craig. "Why Self-Control Is So Important". *The Wooden Effect*. 24 May 2017. Web.

[xix] Araton, Harvey. "Wooden Journeyed Far, Anchored By His Roots". *New York Times*. 5 June 2010. Web.

[xx] Elderkin, Phil. "John Wooden: Lessons for basketball and life". *The Christian Science Monitor*. 5 June 2010. Web

[xxi] Elderkin, Phil. "John Wooden's view from retirement on basketball, discipline". *The Christian Science Monitor*. 12 March 1986. Web.

[xxii] JT, Richard. "John Wooden: the Greatest College Hoops Coach of All Time". *Bleacher Report*. 4 March 2010. Web.

[xxiii] Hyman, Mervin. "A Press That Panics Them All". *Sports Illustrated*. 6 December 1965. Web.

[xxiv] Davis, Seth. "Revisiting the remarkable legacy of John Wooden, the greatest coach of them all". *Sports Illustrated*. 8 March 2017. Web.

11522024R00083

Made in the USA
Lexington, KY
12 October 2018